Ella
es

Ella es

Alegria Zuluaga

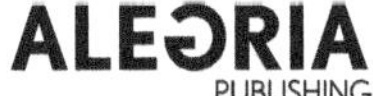

Library of Congress Control number: 2021917599

ISBN: 978-1-7361496-8-3

Published by Alegria Publishing
Book cover and layout by Carlos Mendoza

Foreword

I still remember being 18, fresh out of high-school, and being terrified of turning 20. In the blink of an eye, I was 25, had a job and had travelled to more countries than I could have ever imagined.

I closed my eyes again, and I found myself getting married, starting over in the States, and being a year away from turning 30.

"Will I have a daughter, or a son?" is a question that randomly pops in my head from time to time - something that my 18-year-old-self would have never bothered to ask.

Though I try to make a conscious effort to live in the present, I sometimes cannot help but to think what my future kids are going to look like given their American-Colombian mixed background. What will they think? What will they bring into this world to leave it better than generations before them?

Sometimes, I even wonder what advice I will give my kids when they ask rough and raw questions about life, love, and more.

As I read Alegría's poems, I had one of those moments. You know, where everything clicks. An "aha moment!" as Americans call it. An expression I adopted myself, even when speaking in Spanish – I guess that is what emigrating to a new country does to you.

I realized that this is a book I want my future kids to read while they navigate this serendipitous scenario we call life.

Alegría's poems are a compilation of stories told from the heart and inspired by the soul. This is a book I would have gifted my 18-year-old self, as it captures everything I would have told that clueless version of me in a raw, yet beautiful, way.

Ana Fenley

Writer, editor, blogger, wife.

Dedicated to the woman I was and to the woman I will become.

Dedicated to you, wherever you may be in your journey of life and love.

May love always guide your path, no matter how stormy it may seem.

Preface

Píntate un bosque y piérdete- so that's what I'm doing.
I am climbing, running, skipping, and tripping at times.
All towards a dream, that dream you may ask?
Well- you are holding it in your hands.

Ella es is a poetry collection of my heart, my soul, and my mind. The earth, wind, and fire elements of me, Alegría, a young Colombian, Mexican, and Indonesian woman. My *cultura* is the portion I am always picking up and putting together like jigsaw puzzle pieces. These are the parts of me I have molded together into little birds to set free.

The joy and sorrow that held onto me at my most motivated hours are now typed out and stamped out by ink on paper. This is a collection of lessons I've learned in heartbreak, heart mending, and falling in love with myself through continual cycles of growth. My precious moments of what if's and what happened, bound into this poetry book; I will never forget.

This crazy idea I have unconsciously manifested since my high school days is now printed word for word, bound up and placed in your hands. I spoke of my dreams, and they never included writing. They always included traveling, teaching abroad, singing on stage, and at times being an eternal hopeless romantic.

Well, those are still parts of my life; *Ella Es* is another, because I am a writer.

I wrote this book to feed my alter ego, my femme fate, this ethereal package of disaster and desire I have kept close.

I wrote this book to my younger self, a little sister, my past life as a siren waiting in the water hungry for enlightenment.

I wrote this book for myself. I wrote this book for you.

I wrote this book even though I am still young and learning. I can move on with the lessons I have learned with a little more knowledge and integrity then I started out with.

I wrote this book for you, you mysterious lover, because no matter how many lovers you have scattered around the world, you are never whole until you are grounded in your self worth.

I wrote this for you, you beautiful soul yearning for some sparkle in your tunnel of existential worries.

I write this book for you, no matter who you are because we are all Light, Love, and Fairy Dust.

"I am not looking for perfection, only perseverance"

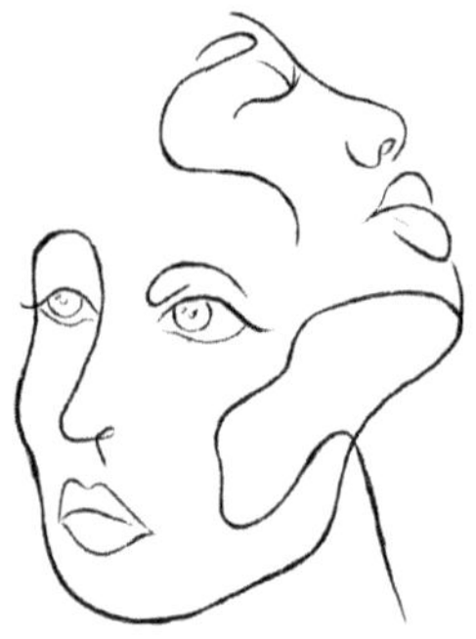

Ella
es

Ella es una caricia al corazón
Y la lluvia más dulce
que calla entre las nubes más fuertes y oscuras
Ella nace de los momentos frágiles y difíciles
Y es descendiente del Sol y la Luna
Ella es hija del mar y de la tierra más negra
Ella es un espíritu que uno se encuentra
en los pequeños momentos
de fe
y de alegría

ella sabe a melancolía
ella es un recuerdo de amor
ella es resistencia y delicadeza
ella es una tormenta hacia al rencor
ella pone a los guerreros de rodillas
y a los pájaros a cantar
ella es una serenata para el alma
ella es una risa entre mamá e hijo
ella es el amor dentro del corazón
ella es una voz
un amor
ella es

No soy de aquí,
ni de allá

I am a daughter of an immigrant
and the granddaughter of immigrants.
A diverse set of stories brought them here;
love and struggle were labored, and I was born.
My name is Alegria, Joy, Happiness,
the emotion that brings sunshine and butterflies
after stormy skies.
My father named me this without knowing;
I would become the eye of the storm.
"No soy de aquí ni de allá."
My brown eyes, round face, broad nose,
and curly locks are all me.
Latina and Pacific Islander- my roots
unapologetically take up the world.
Time continues to grace me
with the confidence to embrace that space.
Even though I try to stay grounded.
I get lost with my head in the clouds
most days- dreaming.
No soy de aquí, ni de allá
Clean out your ignorance and read some history
If the books cannot teach you
Here-

I am your living ministry
I am fetishized but never enough
So, I create my own space
Sit down, it's gonna be a while
While I tell you all of my names
I am the daughter of immigrants
so don't tell me to go back
I'll be here, and over there
All over this *mundo,*
so just be aware
I cannot choose between colonizers and enslaved,
because that beautiful tragedy is how I was made
You cannot blanket my being
I am vibrant
And if that's too loud for you
Well- at least you cannot deny that- I am living proof
My ancestors' blood and energy is saved
On a country that was built on the backs of slaves
If you are uncomfortable with my being
Just know I have sacred divinity protecting me
I am passionate and fearless
I AM ME
No soy de aquí, ni de allá
Mixed and all
I will never fit in
Always breaking your mold
So no
I am not "American"
I am everything all at once
I embrace it all - Always with love

Challenge

The complexity of your tongue
overwhelmed me in thought
the pure substance that sustained me
for years is my name
the proclamation indoctrinated in
my face was extracted from a simple yet so
radical
a choice yet so necessary to live
My name essentially of my lips in
which my hips could never reflect
the idea has been implemented from
the beginning of time
the challenge that I have tirelessly
tried to conquer
these young years have reared me
into exhaustion
Naturally, I wanted the brown skin
my culture has promised me
the large hips that would embody
my lover and increscent my newborns
Naturally, I wanted to feel like I
belonged carrying a flag that fulfilled my
questions of my own history
the challenge has been sewing up the
holes in my *bandera*

the struggle was wrapping my shapeless young
body into the comfort of one flag
    to breathe the scents of one tierra
    yet my hands, my eyes, my feet are the retaliation
    My mind is the confused compass that the wind
pushes and pulls me one way or another.
    Time is unforgiving, and my skin constantly tries
to overcome this challenge
    but it is an apology note that shows through my
fake tan
    all my sides mark me up as if I am what is wrong
    but my fear seized when I remind myself that I am
beautiful in every way
    The tears and frustration disassembled and
deteriorated into nothingness
    and until all the lands merged into one
    filling the holes of my *banderas*
    and smothering me into my name
    the proclamation that fully entitles me
    Alegría

You

Loving you was easy but painful
I know I can be so faithful
But when it came to
        being loyal where it counted
I was left-
Abandoned
Opened my heart
Robbed
        but I gave it away
Never knew my heart was gone
Until my pulse escaped me
I decided that today
I claim what was mine
            and not what was ours

Because that just left me feeling like a coward

I don't spit hurt in the mirror anymore
        Just love
Love me a little more
Smile in the mirror at my beauty marks
You know-
The ones you told me to cover-up
Hold my heart
The heart you wouldn't dare to touch
Love on my curls, the ones you pulled straight
Love shouldn't be hard to seek
It should just overflow, queen
What do you think?
Smile at my heart because that heart is gorgeous
Sorry I lost you
But I hear you
You are seen
You are more than welcome here, queen

Angel
Fly

She flew far away
To see another day
She flies with the angels
to see who she could save
Loving herself was a search unresponsive
So to find the voice
she decided
To fly with the wind
the birds
and the bees.
Tapping into her body that was not at ease
It was a matter of mind
Oh how did she forget how to breathe
Seeking herself in a higher divinity
Opening her eyes through rana dots energy
A journey to be accounted for

Sana sana culito de rana
si no sanas hoy sanaras mañana

Frozen in time,
she saw her soul at play
The child like being
protected by
A Chullachaqui mystery

The never ending stories of horrors her mind believed
Witnessing the power in her possession
She learns to give her stories loving lessons
Embracing the stories that adore her
and let the ones go that don't serve her
all the pain she has morphed into growth
She saw it there strong with a billowing cloak
All the love she has yet to show

Petals
of Hope

Flower petals along the dirt road

A lovely story to be told
But a long one full of hope
She had yet to find out how to grow
Planting seeds along the road

The lovely story unfolds
Branches sprout in plan to escape
Questioning her own fate
Managing a way to reach the light
Basking in the sun with delight

The lovely story unfolds
It's time for her to let those walls crumble and go
To see herself in the reflection glass

Happy endings never die
Because her happiness is found inside

Alas

Cheers to tomorrow's blessings
She rediscovered the best thing
The smile in the mirror
The golden heart she carries in her
Her happiness is wealth
Purpose had led her to fly
To see yet another day
To find the beauty in all divine ways

Free
fall

Let's free fall until we fly
I'll sing a tune for a little while
Carry my heart on my sleeve
It was just a grand opening
Let's free fall until we fly
It's you and me so let's not lie
There is a little fear in this mile
I found the sweetness in your smile
It's you and me for a while
      Sweetness
There has never been a time
where I can rest my mind
I think about you all the time
I never loved nobody
      more than you
      My sweet little angel fly
         My sweet little angel fly

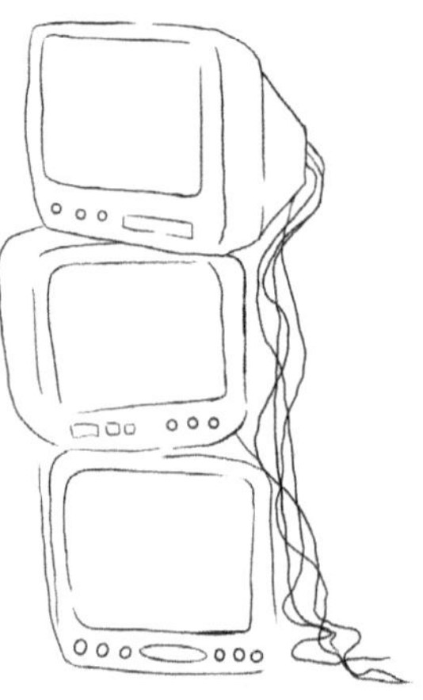

"We live in a world full of expectations.
We live in a world of imaginary things.
We aren't concerned with reality,
Only what we expect reality to be."

Road
less traveled

I shall take the road less traveled
The unfamiliar path
"Let's go"

All I know is that I cannot stay
Wallowing in this valley
Cradled by complacency

All I know is that something inside of me is telling me

"Let's go"

I will walk with a head high
as I climb to the mountain and sky
To stretch as far as the universe goes
Stretch my spine into darkness
Where creation is being born
Among the stars I will get lost
I will make quick and calculated turns
Learning from the stars as they burn
I will move slow as I dive
deep
Deep into darkness
For the ocean holds me close
Reminding me what it was like to breathe

I will encounter rivers and streams that take me
But the energy within my heart will always save me
It will take me
to my home
on the road of the less traveled

"Me voy"

Anxiety

Why do you come to me
You sit like a queen in the space of my mind
I look at the open door
The shattered promises we have left behind
Late emails
Dirty dishes
Dirty laundry
Nervous twitches
Nervous itches

Anxious thoughts come and go
Sometimes they just overflow
As I look at the running faucet
I cannot ignore
The overcompensating
Over explaining
Over thinking
Overstepping my own boundaries

Over
and
over
in
my
mind

I am over it
I am over this
I just want peace
Anxiety
Why do you insist?
Anxiety
Why do you persist?
You have held me captive in my own home
and the only way out
The only way I know how to deal with you
is to explode
Break you with my words
Soften you with a smoke
Grind you with my teeth
Calm you with a toast
Anxiety
You are part of me
But you are only a guest

Never permanent only temporary
So please feel free to sit yourself up with a calming tea
cleanse with intentionality
Indulge within present moment
Nourish with positive energy

Anxiety
leave me be
With a pen and paper
So I can set you free
You are not chained to me
I will not be tainted by your existence
Only
Build
With you
        as my witness

"What does not belong to me, I set free.
What belongs to me will come divinely"

Magical Woman

She is the sunrise
and sunset
All the beautiful things
You have barely met
Strangers in chaos
Tenderness between sheets
It was never
Just the simple things
Always complex beings
Love
She's not easy
Always skipping heartbeats
Always pushing a dream
You were just a glimpse away
From something beautiful and sweet
     Love is patient
        But never sleeps
        She's all the love you have yet to meet

Háblame alma
Porque a veces
Desapareces
Me dejas sola
Con ella
Me atormenta
Me miente
Ella miente
Mi mente
Miente

¡Es una mentirosa!

Me dice cosas que no son lindas
Háblame alma
Sé que estás aquí
A veces siento
Que no estamos conectadas, alma
¿Por qué te vas?
Yo te hago caso
Pero háblame
Dime que estamos bien
Estoy aquí
Esperando tu respuesta
Estoy cansada
De estas voces en mi cabeza
Contando historias falsas
Estoy cansada
    igual que tú
Estoy aquí
Pacientemente
Esperando
    Que regreses a mi cuerpo
Alma
    Regresa a casa

Háblame
alma

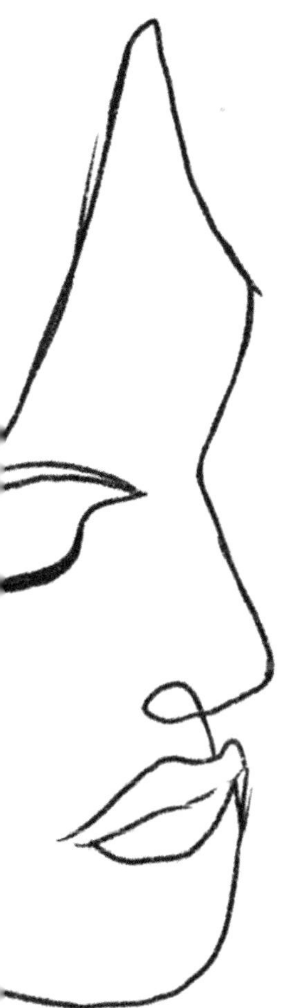

Talk to me
alma

Talk to me alma
Because sometimes you disappear
You leave me alone
With her (my Mind)
She torrements me
She lies to me
My mind lies...

She's a liar!

She speaks of ugly things
Talk to me alma
I know you are here
I know there is a disconnect with you
Alma
Where are you going?
I will listen to you
But talk to me
Tell me we are going to be ok
I am here
Waiting for your response
I am tired of these voices in my head.
I am tired of my mind and these false narratives
Same as you
I am here,
Patiently
Waiting
To come back to this body
Alma
Come back home

Divinity
of Another Life

They couldn't help but to see
The light in her eyes was a distraction to strangers
Her smile seemed contagious
Her kindness was unexplainable
Nothing seemed foreign
All too familiar
Though we have known her for centuries
Loved her for many lifetimes
Lost her
But alas

    Alas
        Alas
            They found the light once more

Past Lives

Recurring past experiences
Lives I have forgotten
The "what has been"
Retraining my mind to transcend
A tunnel of light to tend

Falling onto worlds
Far among this lens
I believe my stories of memory
Of what was meant and supposed to be
A truth I cannot hide
The pain I have endured in past lives
I was born to remember
Born with the knowledge I cannot deny
Medicina ancestral
Takes me to places I remember from my life
Medicina ancestral
Blesses me to remember the stories
I had once lived and denied

"What would my higher self do?"

It is
what it is

I'll leave you broken
like a jar that was too hard to open
I'll leave you like a broken glass
No, don't touch it
It's broken
I'll leave you like rose petals
Scattered across a broken heart
It's not a work of art
It's a much stronger march
It's a million voices on a broken system
It's a tremble inside that doesn't want to listen
It's a happy ending without a proper goodbye
It's a sad letter wanting to die
It's a scary rush that made it out alive
It's a beehive of workers without a concept of reality
It's dreams deferred for the mounds of money
It's a child learning to play
It's a gangster running away
It's an elderly looking for ways
But we keep running on minutes
Relying on hours
Paying our way
Craving a fate
We never stop learning
We just keep on burning this energy
Keeping up symmetry
On this ugly face
It's frustrating, yeah
Never-ending
Finding grace in our age
Finding peace in our graves
Finding love to fill in the days
Just to say,
This is life

Dancing
eyes

Do I overwhelm you?
Do I excite you?
Mysterious eyes danced with the light
Kissed her dreams every night
Although she felt a century was behind her
The timeline had just begun to write her
Her eyes were like butterflies
Flirting with innocent surprise
A beautiful mind inside
Hands intertwined
Presence of a sweet lullaby
The energy of a million miles
Found peace in every breath
Filling her lungs with memory
Calm presence in her galaxy
All meant to be
All set free
All supposed to be
You- my happy being
Being of light
Higher self enveloped in dreams

Pretty
Patience

You can't touch me.
It's ok
One day you will be able to see
She learned that the best ones wait
She learned that the lovers can be tricked by easy bait
She learned that she is exquisite taste
She's open and full of love
She's learned that only certain tongues can taste
That her heart is adorned with thorns
earned from a quick embrace
Enchantress, the boys named her
Goddess, the men never played her.
As she grew into a woman,
The young fools showed to fail her
The fancy clothes and expensive taste
Was only for a short circuit spark
Never for real electricity
Feminine and masculine energy
Roots dig deep
Raw real divinity
Yin and yang energy
Only the real will recognize
That a soul can fly with fate
They are the ones who have truly been hypnotized
By her strong serenity
The one will understand
Her love was built on that divine that never breaks

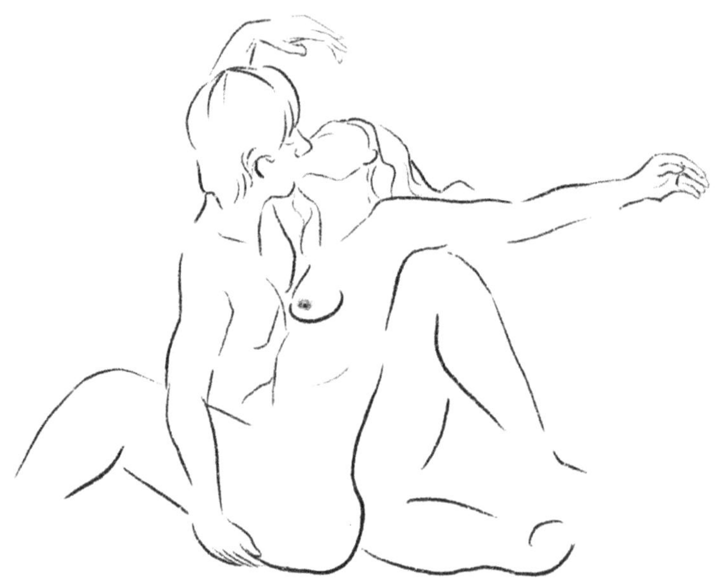

¡Que rico!

Dentro de mis piernas
Cerca de ti
Mirando tu cara
Me haces sonreír
Cada vez que te miro
Me haces sentir
Los nudos en mi corazón
Sabes como destruir
Calienta mi pecho con el tuyo, amor
Te quiero tener cerca
Siempre a mi alrededor

Promise me

The light in her eyes was the love you lived by
The strength in her spine was the greatness you stood by
In her weakness
you carried her
In your heart,
you promised her
Never to leave your happiness for another

Te escribo

Te escribo desde mi paraíso
Te veo,
Eres mi vicio,
Creo lo que dices,
Creo en lo que haces,
Soñando contigo,
Soñando mentiras.

Intento curar tus espinas,
Sacándote una sonrisa,
Y me doy cuenta
Que todo es mentira.

Soy víctima de tu amor
Un ciclo de admiración
Y falsas promesas;
Solamente eres un hombre,
Y yo, la mujer que manifiesta.

Te describo en mis sueños,
Eres mis manifestaciones y fantasías,
Eres mi novela con drama
Eres mi príncipe y mi guerrero

Todo lo bueno
Todo lo malo
Eres lo que no sabía que existía.
Te quiero conocer
Te quiero amar
Lo quiero todo de ti.

Rosas con espinas,
Un mar ahogándome de amor
Una mirada de pasión
Y me juzgo
Porque solamente vives en mis sueños.

Tus palabras y tus espinas
Eres un hombre de cuento
Pero sigo escribiéndote desde mi paraíso.

Just a touch

If I could only feel your embrace
I just want a taste
Your divinity
Your faith
It's easy to run and hide,
to just
drop and break
The little promises we have made
to be true and unafraid
I mean that in the best way
I will always go my way
Shine your light on me- Make my day

Goddess
in disguise

She's a goddess in disguise
No compromise
She knows her light

Illuminates throughout the night
She came here to shine bright
She came here to love you right

She's here
She's a delight

Never here to fight
Only to shine her light

Love you through the night
Hold you close
Kiss you goodnight
Lullabies like sirens
Keeping in mind
There's not a time you deny them
Records of a lost time
Lessons of this land
Forgotten time

She's a goddess in disguise
No compromise
She shines her light
Illuminated the divine

Caution

Careful with her lips
They stain thoughts
And those hips
How they will spin you around
     Hypnotizing

She's a divine thing
Her curls fall perfectly
In locs of thought
She will love you 'til the end stops
Love you so you will always remember
     how she grows
Without a warning
Regardless if you are by her side
The petals remain falling
     Remarkable
        Alarming
Here she comes
        Charming
    Blossoming
Evolving
    She will
Bloom
    Bloom
        Bloom

Cherished

She's the light in your darkness
She's high up
Yes, a goddess
Keeping you away
So she can save the day
Finding out your ways
To keep her sane

You can't seem to figure her out
She's an unfinished masterpiece
Not any work of art
She's your lover by night
A warrior by day

She's the sunshine
Even when it rains
She's the window open during the storm
But she's the only love that can keep you warm

She is your light in the darkness
Some say she is a goddess
So, if you leave her
Don't be alarmed
Her energy is not history
Her blessings are eternal mysteries
You will see
As her heart beats as loud as a drum
She will fly like a wild one

Always in your memory
If you entice her to fly free
You will see
    She's a goddess
But she will cherish your heart

Sugar in
the stars

I'm a goddess if I'm quite honest
I feel like a million stars.
Swimming through Venus and Mars
Got love to fall back on
I'm a goddess if I'm quite honest
I never lose control
     Always on a roll
        Kiss me softly
Make your day better
With a smile
Everlasting sweetness
Fountain of Euphoria
It's because
I am your weakness
Keep it between us

Ethereal
fire

Fall
But never break
She learns from her mistakes
Fall
and never shatter
She held her ground with love and angel feathers
    It's the time for courage
        Time for resilience
Time for her mind to finally become
Quiet
She falls quite often
Clumsy and young
Silly and dumb
A volcano of vibrant sexual energy
A hurricane of ethereal mystery
Fall
But never breaks
One day
    one day
        one day
She will rise from these flames

Lo sentí

Lo sentí cuando me dijiste que no
Pero seguí con los encantos
Llamándote desde lejos
No fue mi culpa que saliste a ver
Y cuando nos vimos
Una energía magenta dentro de nosotros dos
Y no podía separarme de tu pecho
De tu corazón
Lo quería robar
sentía paz por primera vez
en los hombros de alguien desconocido
Sentí tus palabras,
Tu sonrisa
Lo sentí en tus besos
Y en cada caricia
me sentí en casa

I Felt it

I felt when you told me no
But I continued with charm
Calling you from afar
It was not my fault you came out to see
And when we saw each other
A magnetic energy between us
I couldn't separate myself from your chest
I wanted to steal your heart
I felt at peace for the first time
in the arms of a stranger
I felt your words
Your smile
I felt it in your kisses
And with every caress
I felt at home

Falling

The rush is alarming
I'm falling
My heart is pounding
You know I'm scared
I've been spared
Tossed on the side
Like a flower
to die
You know real love is there
when you don't want to fight it.
You know love is real when you need to try it
Yeah, your heart is pounding
Face gets flushed
but there are butterflies
You hesitate a little
because you don't want to be hypnotized
When it's all gone
It's the risk we take, falling.
Some people are just worth that trip
"I would rather love you for a little while
than not be able to love you at all"
That's when you know
you just have to take the fall.

Amante monolingüe

Amante monolingüe
Me siento completamente,
Enamorada
Quiero olvidarte
Y parece imposible.
No me siento sola
Pero, corres por mi mente
Cada día en el trabajo
Y apareces en todos mis poemas
¡Los escribí para ti, bobo!

Sé que no entiendes,
y ojalá, no quieras hacerlo.

Te comprendo,
No sé cómo vas a reaccionar
Pero lo sientes en el pecho
Cada vez que te miro
Me interpretas perfectamente,
Mas no a mi poesía.

*bobo: term of endearment; stupid

As we are

As I am
Close to you.
I feel our hearts collide
I have been hiding
Putting up a front

I am honest
And I am blunt
I didn't want anything to do with you
But you conquered my heart so soon
Without a fighting chance
You made plans

And I am falling
Falling into the look in your eyes
Yes, your smile
It's cheesy to say
But you make me laugh
Laugh at the possibility that this is even reality

That I found a part of my heart within you
When I told you I loved you
I didn't say this out of kindness
I said this from my lioness within
The part of me that wants to reach heaven

You N Me

You and me
Infinite beings
You aren't the angel face that I found in my dreams
You are the rough rugged man I held in my sleep
And even though a decade apart
You hold me like a work of art
With tenderness so strong
Loving you never felt wrong
Love me until the moon is ripe
Love me until our time finds the light
In this chaos
We promised to be united
Our timing was not invited
But baby with you I'm delighted
Flying like a bird
Knowing if I get hurt
I have your arms to rest in
Baby our time is precious
Found you in my dream
So I treasure this
If loving you was so easy
I'd be a fool in love once more
But it's ok because I know this chaos is worth fighting for

Labios

Labios
Tus labios me llamarán lentamente
cerca de ti,
Labios
Dame un espacio
¿Puedes compartir?
Tengo curiosidad.
Cerca de ti
Cerca de tu corazón
Qué bonito cuando me estés amando
Qué bonito fuera que algún día me amaras
Ojalá me amaras en mis tiempos antiguos
en mis tiempos malos y amargos
y en mis tiempos bonitos y apasionados
Ojalá me amaras
hasta mi último respiro
y a nuestros labios regresar
para compartir nuestro primer beso
Te amo

Tu olor me hace algo
Me pone los pelos de punta
Que se acelere el corazón
Me haces algo cariño
Y no sé cómo lo haces
Ni por qué me lo haces

Quién soy yo para juzgar tus sueños
Tienes mi permiso de soñar libre
Porque sueño contigo cada noche
Y como fueron nuestros momentos débiles

El camino hasta mis labios
Fue duro
El camino hasta mi pecho
Suave
Y Pues
Tus manos explorarán el resto

¿Y el resto qué será?   Olor
Jugoso y Mojado
paso a paso
El camino hacia el peligro

Dentro de mis piernas
Cerca de mí
Dentro de mí
Quiero acariciar
Tu cuerpo entero
Que me guarda   Con mi dulzura
Que me protege   Entretente conmigo
Entra   Y nuestra energía única
Dentro de mí   Manteniéndote cerca
    Entretengámonos   Entreteniéndote cerca
        Deliciosamente   Adentro de mí
                               Ven
                               Sueña
                               Estoy aquí - Libre

Memory

Channel our energy
It sings a certain frequency
Vibe with our love
Sing me a song
The sweet words of kindness
Words that never blind us
We are one
Combine the sweetness of many
Like a sacred recipe
Yin and yang
Female masculine energy
I am one with you
You are one with me
Leave us with sweet memories

Muse de amor

Nothing seems scary
When time melts away
Kindness is not astray
Can you be the one that stays?
I didn't want to miss you
Trying to forget your face
But
in your arms
I find grace
As our overflowing cups fill our days
With laughter and youth
I am your muse
In your heart
I planted a seed of light
Despite our different timing
It just seemed right
You adore my mind
You are my muse
Painting this moment ripe

Angel Feathers

Our love was built from tragedy
My heart shattered repeatedly
We found a new reality
Never thought this was supposed to be

Found our love between the rubble
Holding this house in trouble
I knew for a fact this all stings
but you make my heart sing

Kissing you repeatedly
Cut like nostalgia baby
I wish to be around ya
God held us closer
Mending all the pieces
Your touch left me bolder
To make it a little better

Our love was built from angel feathers
Found pieces of you and me
Chaos of tradition
Was never the mission
But we found ourselves tangled
In love without fear

Angels watch to guide us near
And kiss the ones we love
Holding this newfound family tighter

We are meant to be
Fate and destiny
Weren't designed perfectly
But I found you and me
Profound blessings
Are always meant to be

A light-filled tunnel
between the thunder
You are full of wonder
Between two eyes
Divinity and light
You shine so bright

Deeper

He says to go deeper
As if I have a fear of diving
I have lived in the depths my whole life
Never hiding
Only for you to bring me to surface
To feed me a breath of fresh air
With that long and loving stare

No way I can compare
My soul to yours
But we seem to fly above the clouds
    like birds

I was meant to go deeper
    not desperately
You can go on your way
and I will continue on mine
I will let you go
because I am not blind
Don't expect me to break you apart
looking for a wounded child inside

I am loyal
I am faithful
I love hard
I love deep
I love my way

I fly like free birds, whose song echoes in the
rain
I rebirth peacefully, like butterflies in my brain
I grow like deep roots, embracing black soil
The fruits I birth are sweet, never spoiled
My growth isn't afraid of depths or experiencing
highs
Because I always land in the divine light

I am not afraid to go deep
But maybe you are with me
I will let you fly
Every so peacefully
Prove me wrong if you so please
I will continue loving you from the depths of my
needs
And doing what brings me liberty

Not it

Cleaning up my act
This is a fact
Eventually at night
I close my eyes tight
I think of you close to me
Breathing into me
Something makes me crazy
Almost on the daily
I promised I would try to forget
But I guess I've lost that bet
Adding fuel to my fire
I never stopped burning
Adding light to my nights
I keep yearning
For your breath to become my air
How I miss your long loving stares
Trying to forget you there
Next to my morning hair
You never cared
We just shared the sweetest moments with the morning sun
Now I'm trying to remember why you weren't "the one"

Uncertainty

Maybe
Maybe it's the way you look in my eyes
Holding me down as I move through the night
Just maybe if I didn't want to run
We would have some kind of fun
Maybe
If I felt
That I wanted be held
We would defy odds
and come up with some fairytale
Just maybe
But for me
I cannot see
If this is even meant to be
Because what I have constructed
from the ideals of this society
Is that our love cannot be a reality
As I see in you
A heart of precious gold
As I see in me
A heart that wants to explore
As I see
In us
Open and full of trust
My mind isn't writing down these words
I am serving my soul and what she prefers
How the words written down on this page
Are manifestations being claimed
I find my way in your presence
I find myself trying to accept that
Our love may not be ordinary
But it is wild and extraordinary

Thank you,
Adiós

I know you probably don't think of me
I know this is my fantasy
I just want to let you know
I still love myself around you
I still think of you
I can't thank you enough
Not even for your *besos* or your touch
Just for your trust
For pushing me into this freefall
and for having faith in me to fly
When I was not even sure why I had wings
Thank you for letting me be
Thank you for loving me

- Darlin' Z

False
Promises

My energy is on a battlefield
Feelings went to soar
I knew the sweet talk was just words
until you kissed me as if I've never been kissed before
I hate myself and this open-heart surgery
Because I was never meant to be
Just another conquest story
Loving you was the hardest thing to do
Because I knew I'd get played
Toyed like a fool
Sink in your words
Melt in your arms
I wish that this felt like every other love song
But you're not my Prince Charming
Just another disguise,
Just a man
Wrapped up
So nicely in lies

*"She's no longer here
To lick the wounds that came before her
To applaud you after simple apologies
She is no longer here to give bloody beating hearts
She is no longer here to hold your pain
when it gets too heavy for you to carry
She's no longer here"*

Forgotten
Left like a bookmark on the climax point
  Forgotten
Like water boiling on the stove
  Forgotten
Like a burning match left to die
  Forgotten
Promises were words-simply
  Forgotten
Our energy exploded with every encounter
I was your arm candy at every social affair
I gave you grace
Cleaned up your face
All simply
  Forgotten
Families met
and we fell deeper in love
Young souls absorbing energies
How extremely fun
All now
  Forgotten
Sacrifices we made
Sacrifices we planned
We wanted to stay
   and stay
You said
  you would do what it takes
I stayed
  I stayed
     You
    You
  You
Flew.
  I was

Forgotten

"Soulmate"

Summer
Love

Unforgettable
Wine stains on her skirt, a hot summer evening
She looked like sunshine
Tasted like ocean salt
She was made of tears and laughter
Her heart held lots of love
She looked at the scene
Like a work of art
It was the ocean breeze
That grew them apart
She left
And that's when summer ended
The days grew colder
Light began to fade from the hours
She was a light in his life
But he never felt enough to fight
They tell you, if you love someone let them go
So he watched her walk into the setting sun

Call Me

Call me selfish
That I'm on my own
Call me a liar
That I wanted this time to roam
Call me sad
When I wanted your embrace
Call me immature
When I wanted just a call
Call me greedy
Because you were everything I wanted and more
Call me a romantic
Because I chose your louve
Call me ignorant
Because I ignored all the signs that called
Call me love
Because I will always remain
Call me darling
Call me by my name

I didn't listen
I didn't listen to your heartbeat when it spoke to mine
My walls were up, and I had to deny
That I was running into you in my dreams every night
It was like a spell you had over me
Holding me tight

You swept me off my feet
Held me and kissed me sweet
You built a bridge for my bare feet
Strong and study
I didn't believe I was worthy

I broke it with the weight of my secrecy
How did I do this to you?
How did I do this to myself?
Why did I hurt you?

Hurt us and stomp down selfishly
If I was your bridge
I thought I'd be strong
Carry you on

But if I was your bridge
It would tremble and break
I never imagined
you
you
You would keep holding onto me
As I release all my weight
I must plaster the cracks and put the boards back in place
Because one day
one day
We will walk together across that bridge I broke

I will repair it as I face my weakness
I will repair it as my heart is depleted
I will repair it as my hands keep bleeding
I will repair it until our souls are at peace

I have never asked for so much mercy
I know you don't believe me
But I can't help but to feel
The weight of my deceit

All the lies I told myself and to you
All I want is for this bridge to be brand new
All I want is me and YOU

I want your soul to speak to me too
Because our souls know each other so well
I can't believe
I lied to myself
I didn't listen to your heart
when it spoke to mine
I wanted so badly to control time
my ego too enveloped my mind
My young foolish siren dragged me out of line
Livid and hell
I fell
And brought you with me
When all you did
Was build a bridge for me
To stand strong on my feet
When my actions brought me down
to my knees.

Broken
Bridges

Ella *es*

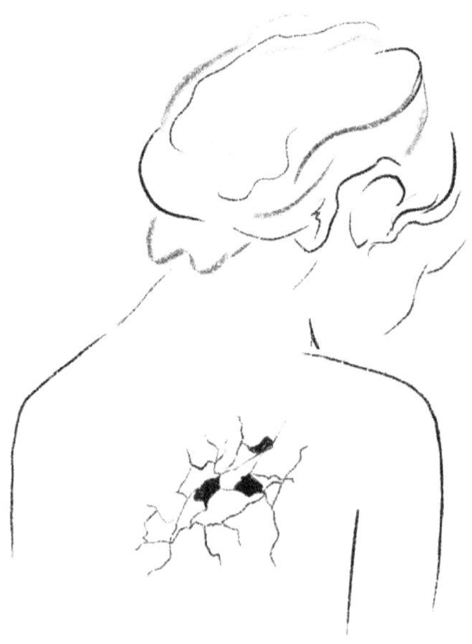

Broken
Heart

    The heart that once palpated for joy
as the eyes, soul, and mind once connected to something
miraculous, now for a moment in time
-pauses.
    The butterflies that flooded in your body now leave.
    The adrenaline rush that pushed blood in a rapid
flow now seizes and tenses.
    Your heart pauses- now abrupt palpitations.
    That is when you realize the reality
and your perception has been shattered.
    That is when you come face to face,
with a broken heart.

To my little sister after a heartbreak

Little baby girl
One day you will learn
That these tears are ok
These tears one day will fade
Sleepless nights will turn to days
But for right now the pain is all too real
You will miss him tenderly
Miss how he feels
Just be sweet
Little baby girl
I know it's a tough world
But the only thing I know for sure
is what hurts and heals is
Love!
Always be sure
You have yourself
I'm sorry you couldn't contain a river of tears
It gets better; at least, that's what I hear
I'm sorry you had to see some tears
But one day you'll know
that the love you carry is all too real
That love is absolutely real
And love truly heals

Racetrack

It's easy to go fast
When Life seems like a racetrack
It's easy to choose one night stands
When your bed feels so cold at sunset
But when you get completely comfortable
with the warmth of your own body
Embracing the sheets all to yourself
until you rise with the sun
For a moment
    you pause.
    You aren't on the run

Loneliness doesn't exist when peace
with yourself is a blessing

Nothing is needed
Lust is convenient
love is patient
It's just a mindset of give and take
And choosing yourself at the end of the day.
Because it's ok to be with- me, myself, and I
Because we are together until we die.
There's no race for that
It's just self-love
And the romance
    will be on track

Mourning with Espíritus

Late mornings
Baptizing my face with tears
The sun touching my skin from the windows
Begging me to leave my house
The house that filters dark spirits that dance in the
corners of my eyes
Despite the palo santo I burn at night
The shadows persist with questions
        I am afraid
I know that they are here to tell me things
I am not equipped with the tools to keep going
I just don't want to hear the messages that are looking at
me in the mirror

My body creaks as my feet hit old wooden floors
Creaking in sympathetic symphony
I drag myself in and out of doors
It takes everything from my being to move
I have been without energy
Famished as I wake
Every morning craving some strength
When I appear in the world
I smile faltered grace
Holding my own desires of being alone and loved close
to me
Like the child I never nurtured, crying out for me
I know you see me
Espíritus
But I just want to disappear
There aren't enough hours in the day for me to tell you
how I feel

I take showers in the afternoon and drift off to places
In the sounds of water hitting my skin like tiny bullets
and blessings
Temporarily offering a shallow sense of touch
I think about how I wish to hibernate myself in my
books and never leave home

With the same itch of leaving the house and digging my
toes in the sand
I punish myself with the desire of doing everything
And in turn
Doing nothing at all

Casa

Siento una soledad muy tranquila
Nadie me dijo
Que se puede sentir tan rico
Porque todo el mundo
Se va por la vida estudiando una puerta
Y no está abierta
Pero si te das cuenta que
la casa no tiene paredes
Ni piso
Esas cosas tú las necesitas construir
Menos mal que
Tú lo haces como tú quieres
No dependes
De ninguna persona
Diciéndote que así no se hace
Tú lo puedes hacer como te gusta
Es tu casa
      son tus puertas
           Es tu vida
No tienes tiempo para esperar a nadie que te ayude
Y después
Puedes celebrar en tu casa
Con una familia y llena de amigos

Addiction

My hands ache from loving you
It's like an addiction
I never signed up for you
But you show me too

I am an artist with lots of views
My hands ache from loving you
It's ascending into something new

I love the way you make me feel
Floating in this pleasurable way
Getting done what I have to say
Make it sad or on a sunny day

Our relationship was never on display
Never perfect
Never the same
I wish to love you every day
But sometimes you loathe the things I say
And sometimes you just run away
But with time I'll put you on display
I'll love and nurture you in every way
To love the way you make me feel
You make me fly when I need to heal

¡Letras!

Letras en mi cabeza,
que suenan como una canción
brincando con certeza;
una serenata entre mis sueños,
y por momentos, te veo entre mis poemas.
Brincan, corren, brillan, vuelan.

Saltando sobre las paredes,
a la orilla de la ventana,
frente a mi cara.

Corriendo,
escapando de los gritos,
y los tiros que pasan detrás de mí.
Paro y digo: "¡Soy suficiente!"

Vuelo,
escapando de lo que siento,
mi sangre no deja de correr,
mi piel me fue infiel,
mi piel, me espanta a veces.

¡Escúchame!,
detente,
respira…
No nos hagas daño,
brillas con cada respiro,
vuelas con tu propia inspiración.

Estoy aquí,
¿te acuerdas de mí?,
soy parte de tu alma,
y juntos, construiremos sueños.

Poco a poco,
antes de que cierres los ojos,
viajaremos por los astros y la Tierra,
descubriremos dimensiones y largos planos.

Vamos a viajar con tu lápiz y papel,
vamos a viajar por la luz y oscuridad,
vamos a viajar entre tu piel y sangre,
vamos a viajar entre tus tormentas y fantasías.

No te olvides de mí,
que canto por tu amor,
y entre tus memorias más profundas,
a veces los poemas,
desaparecen por la incertidumbre.

No tienen nombre,
no ven la luz,
no les da tiempo de respirar.

Deja que tu alma repose,
deja que tu alma recuerde,
deja que tu alma despierte.

Escribe poco y siente mucho.

Siempre, entre tus venas
y tu poder para crear,
tus mundos,
viviendo, respirando,
volando y brillando.

Free Aura

My aura feels complex
Aren't we all a mess sometimes?
Just gotta write it out
Or better
Speak it from that closed mouth
Doesn't it feel good?
Singing that poetry
Expelling the pain and setting it free?
It feels good
To let the energy be free
Bring in the positive energy unto me

Mi casa
es su casa

Home.
Nostalgia blows through my mind when I think of you.
When life gets scary I close my eyes and hold on tight.
To remember you.
Breathing in, and breathing out.
Calma
Eres mi pequeño pedazo de paraíso e infierno
Eres todo lo que soy
Eres parte de mí
En esta vida o en otra
Pero cada vez
Me siento
En Casa

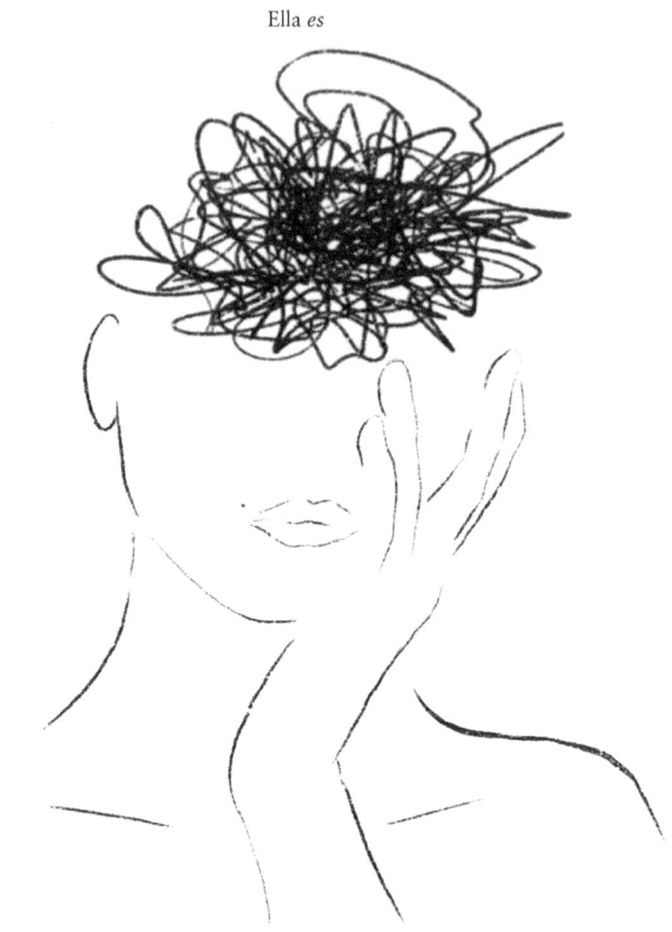

Ahogando

Sanando las espinas que me mostraste
Cultivando el dolor que tenías
Levantando la oscuridad
Y se me fue encima
Como lluvia
No lo podía parar
Tratando de nadar
Ahogándome

Pachamama

You fill me with your darkest moment
Asking for mercy
Asking for forgiveness
You fill me with death
Expecting life
I am too powerful for your ignorance
I carry more knowledge greater
than your predictions
You fill me with hate
Expecting me to love
You fill me with nothingness
Expecting me to grow

Como Storni

Llevo mi corazón al mar
Para recargar
Lo que tenía vacío
Mi energía
Dulcemente dañada en manos que no quería
A veces mi corazón
Estaba en manos que herían
Para dar un poco de gracia
Para sacar una sonrisa a la vida
Dañando en manos que no quería

Y aquí estoy
Recargando las baterías
Juntito al mar como Alfonsina
Escribiendo poesía
sacando mis penas
Con cada palabra que escribo
Veo los poemas perdidos entre las olas

Aquí estoy
Tratando de recargar mis baterías
Poniéndome mis pilas
Reconociendo
Lo que tenía
Reconstruyendo
    Lo que quería
        Lo que tenía

Lo que tengo
    Adentro de mí
        Adentro de mí

Memorias que sufría
Y en una constante tormenta
Reconociendo cosas que no servían
Reviviendo memorias que perdía
De mi vida
    Y tiemblo
        De miedo
            De rabia
              Y
De Alegría

Aquí estoy escribiendo mi vida
Esta parte del mar
es mi pequeño paraíso e infierno
Donde llevo a mi corazón
Mi alma
    Mi cuerpo
        Y doy luz
            A mi poesía

Sunny days

When everything seemed like it was going to be ok
Sunny days
I was high on your shoulders, just you and me for the day
Sunny days
Seeing you was the best part of my day
When everything seemed cloudy and gray
Sunny days
You were my lighthouse in the storm
You fought the monsters when I felt alone
Sunny days

You were the silly faces after a scary fight
You were my bedtime kisses almost every night
Night has come
I know I've grown
And in ways you may not like,
but here we are- getting old

Through this journey
I'm reaching mountain tops
The highest heights

Only the ones I could reach
Because I never forgot
How you lifted me on your shoulders
Laughed at my silly mistakes
through the clouds and rain

I wish we could have another sunny day
I wish you could love me where I'm at
I wish you would look at my face
And tell me that you didn't give up

I'm slowly learning
I'm going to fall a lot
But just like my first steps
You were there for that

I'm doing this not only for you
I'm doing this for me too
I'm not always wild and free
But that's just who I am meant to be
Sunny days
Remembering when it was just you and me
I wish the days were simple again you see
Sunny days
On your shoulders
And love
Unconditionally

Heart
Bruise

Sometimes I think my heart stops
I feel like I can't get enough
Oxygen to my lungs
And the tears start to drop
Sometimes I think my heart knows
How deep my pain really goes
Breathing in and out
Until I feel the lights go out
I try hard not to think
Of all the pain
I've caused myself so soon
Of all the pain
I've caused myself for you
It's ok
My heart is black and blue
My heart will heal soon
But my heart will never
Stop loving you

Deleted

I deleted all the photos
I thought it would feel better
But it's hard to snap my fingers
Erasing my life
It's hard to forget
The best days of my childhood
Never a second thought
The best days of my childhood where with you
No matter how rough

Yeah, you have been through some shit
And so have I
But whatever happened
We had each other
    right?
I thought you were a superhero
Disappearing once and awhile
Only to arrive
When I was in despair

Arriving sometimes on time
Sometimes you were by my side
Now you arc ncvcr thcrc
I know you miss me
I pray for you every night

We are connected
   remember?
Connected for life

I deleted all the photos of you
Only to find out
I see you everywhere
I feel like I'm losing this fight
Our egos are big
Yeah I got that from you
I saw your face today
I hope you are alright
I miss you like crazy
Can we give up this fight?

Unforgettable

Somehow my mind finds a way to mourn you
My heart runs back to the ideas
The ideas that are now consumed by the fog of memory
Of what was supposed to be
Of what could've been
Somehow my heart is tugged
by the tsunami in my stomach
Stained by the broken promises now resurfacing
Somehow my heart drowns again
at the thought of lost words
Unforgettable
My mind calms in the chaos of the forbidden

Re-love-ution

Cuántas veces necesito decir.
Esta revolución es algo que pasa por dentro
Solamente nosotros podemos sanar
nuestros- miedos,
           heridas,
                dolor
Consigue tu poder
con cariño
con pasión
con tranquilidad
Guía a tu niño interior
Y míralo crecer en el jardín de tu alma
Volando, sonriendo, jugando en paz
Lucha por la sanación de la gente
Lucha para cultivar tu poder.
Vive
Libre
sin miedo
con amor

It's easier to write about our dreams than the hardest parts of our life. The parts that shaped us into who we are overwhelm us when we revisit them with a pencil. It's easier to write about the fantasies that we have not yet touched; things that have only lived in our imaginations, far fetched from our relative reality. We have to believe that what we touch turns into magic- and is not tainted by our connection to the past. Our perspectives are based on our experiences. It's hard to let go, to release. But in order to create a new, we must surrender, completely surrender to ourselves, to our soul. We do not surrender to the world. We surrender to our soul."

Inner mini me

My soul is a little girl
dressed in frilly dresses and curls
My soul is a little girl
Known to be pure and fully assured
My soul is a little girl
She comes from the cosmos
Laughing and playing among the stars
Doing somersaults on the earth's ground
My soul is a little girl
Careful and rebellious at large
She sings in the rain
And laughs with the sun

Where are you now?
With your undying love for wishing stars

Alma
Where have you gone,
have you been hurt and been wronged?

The world is painful, beautiful, and wild.
All of that spirit encompasses my inner child

It will take me awhile to get back to you
It will take me back to hold you
I am close
I remember your laugh and how you danced by the fire
How your eyes lit up the night
The darkness is here and it's holding me
Tight

Alma mía
I know you are there
I know sometimes I feel empty

Alma mía
But I shouldn't be scared
My night is magnetic; my pain is power
So I reclaim what is ours

Alma mía
Through love
we can connect,
we can remember,
we can rejoice
Alma mía
Estoy aquí
Estamos aquí
Estaremos felices

Alma

Dreams

You are sweet like honey
wild
yet I learn to nurture you with time
dreams
You candidly gift my soul a dose of truth
The truth I walk close to you
My protectors from above
Always know how to love
Open to my faults
Open to walk into my wildest dreams
Because for the longest time-
Dreams
    Dreams
Dreams
you scared me
Flying high above the clouds
Flying high because I am proud
Proud to be
The daughter of the sea and sun
The moon and stars above
I am grounded to love
Carried by faith and my wildest dreams
Carried by courage and never fear
Kiss the ground as I walk
Embracing
Protecting mama pacha with love

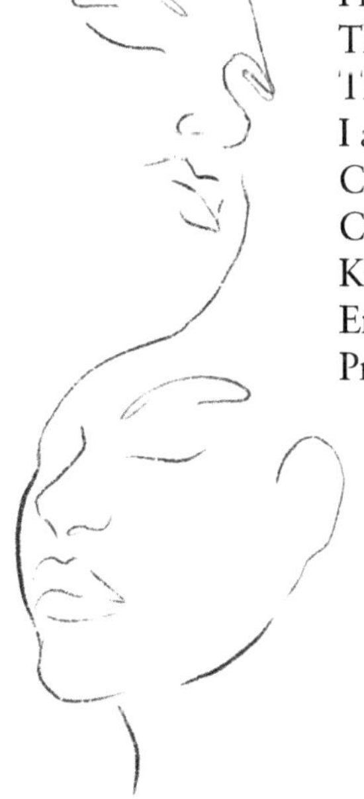

Buscando

Te busco en el aire
Por Dios, ¡Contéstame!
Busco tu voz
En todos los lados extraños
Busco tu mirada
Gritando en el espejo
Esperando contestar mis preguntas

¿Dónde estás?

No queremos repetir los pecados otra vez
No quiero verte con esa pinta* confundida
¿Quién eres?
¿Para dónde vas?

Mírame
Limpia tu espejo
Estoy aquí
Siempre estaré aquí
Esperándote
Tengo fe que vas a estar bien
Pero prométeme que nunca me vas a olvidar
Prométeme que no te irás buscándome qué cosas que no
te sirven
Conoces lo bueno de lo malo
Prométeme que todavía tienes fe
Prométeme que nunca te vas a olvidar de mí
Prométeme que vas a seguir luchando por el amor
Por tu amor
Prométemelo

-Alma

pinta* : look on a face

I promised I'd be there for you, no matter what
I promised I'd give you everything I got
But now I feel
beat
Beaten down by this moment,
this place, this time.
All I can think now is
why Why why
Why can't I serve the ones I love in the same manner?
Why is it just silly telephone chatter?

I can't just hold you and kiss you goodnight
I can no longer sing you lullabies

But I promise you something alright?
I will never say goodbye.

Even though I am here and you are over there
The love I have for you is too much to bear
My love will climb mountains
Swim through rivers
Be tossed by ocean waves
There will never be a day
Where my love for you will break

It's hard to make peace with this world
But everything happens with reasoning

Makes me miss the simple things
Like the way you cooed as I sang you to sleep
Or as you hid to scare me as I walked through the door
I love you little ones
No matter what
I'll be here.
With so much love
I love you.
Everyday a little more.

Little ones

Tiempo

Cuánto tiempo pasará
Sin verte sonreír
Cuánto tiempo pasará
Sin escuchar tu voz
Cuándo vas a llegar a la realidad
¿Cuánto tiempo necesitas?
En estos días se me va acabando la paciencia
En estos días
Hace falta tu sonrisa
En estos días
Hace falta
Alegría

Heavy heart

Heaviness in your chest.
You are running out of breath.
Just woke up from a nightmare
into reality.
It's all a dream
Different dimensions
Feels like a curse
It hurts to recognize
The loneliness
And the hurt
But she's there.
Staring right back
Wanting a response to get her on track
But you are lost for words.
To get her up
To give her breath
All you are trying to do
is dig through your stuff
Looking for happiness.
You lost it.
Find it quick.
Looking for peace
The day has begun
Find it quick.
You are running out of time.

Ancestor call

She speaks to me in an ancient tongue,
Mija.
I have been killed over a thousand years.
speak to me so we shall not forget the magic
speak to me so you will not forget your magic
I have died over and over again for you to breathe.
All the parts of you are now one,
and you too shall die over and over again
until we meet
where the stars kiss the earth's gentle breeze
tell me
What is it like?
What do you see?
How do you feel?
speak to me, and tell me how we can heal.

Eres la nieta de curanderas
brujas que quieren quemar,
pero sigues aquí.
        confundida,
insegura de tu poder
cuéntame mija
cuándo vamos hablar?
estoy aquí
entre los astros y tus pies.
Canta amor cántame otra vez

Broken angels

The pit in her stomach
Her intuition guiding her
Twisting her out of comfort
And shooting out into the stars

She knows how to love
And love she knew well

Sometimes we run into fallen angels
And feel like we know them well
Only see their broken halo

Holding on to them tight
Love resides in each divine soul
Can I hold you upright?
Guiding with light
It has begun
Sometimes the path
is dark and heavy
And we let love light the way
Love is the most resilient
Love never fails
Love always stays

Cuídate

Mi sangre sana
Mi lengua cuida
Mi corazón rompe
Mis ojos hipnotizan

Hechos y directos
Caminando contra la corriente
Mírame por espejos
Mírame no tiembles

Mi cara acaricia
Mi alma ama
Mi mente lucha
Mis manos sienten

Temblé con energía
eléctrica con poder
No me temas
Soy tu amiga
No me temas

Yo te cuido

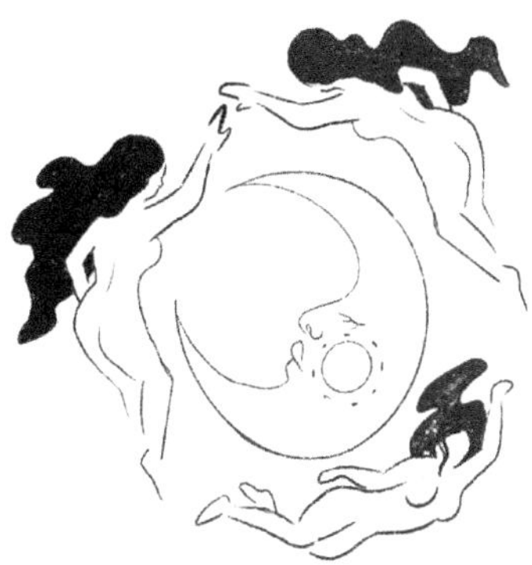

Women

Mujeres
We are the sunbeams dancing on the ocean floor
penetrating and the aura of the unknown
We are the light beams caressing the deep
Never afraid of the dark
Because we birthed that too
Porque la oscuridad es el único referente de la luz.
Because darkness is the only reference to light
Mujeres
We are not afraid of
birthing creation
birthing humanity
We go where we must
We create compassion from fear
We build strength from danger
We evolve scarcity into abundance
We birth peace from wars
Mujeres
We are the daughters, sisters, mothers, *abuelas*,
ancestors ancient energy
We are
Mujeres

Amante
de sueños

Estoy aquí
A tu lado
Con el camino limpio de duda
La luz pasa por tu cara
Un nuevo día
Y estoy aquí contigo
Por suerte eres guapo
Y con cara de buena gente
Por suerte me encontraste
Otro día
Caminando por la vida
Y te encuentro
Otra vez
En mis sueños
Ilusiones
No te conozco
Pero algún día serás
Aquí a mi lado
Compartiendo la madrugada
Y no solamente en mis sueños
Buenos días
Buenas tardes y
Buenas noches
Amante de mis sueños

Te quiero

Quiero acariciar tu pelo cuando hablas
Quiero mirarte como nadie te ha mirado
Quiero conocer tus sueños
y empujarte a cumplirlos
Quiero hacer muchas cosas contigo

No te conozco
pero te quiero amar
porque te amo desde nuestras vidas pasadas

Quiero acariciar tu pelo cuando hablas
Quiero mirarte como nadie te ha mirado
Quiero conocer tus sueños
y empujarte a cumplirlos
Quiero hacer muchas cosas contigo

Ya te conozco
Eres para mí
Ahora simplemente se trata de recorrer el tiempo
Juntos
    Juntos
        Juntos
al fin
no te conozco ahora
no te conozco en este momento

No te conozco.
Solamente vives en mis sueños.
Ojalá algún día-
tus sueños se encuentren
con los míos

Garden

This gaping hole in my heart goes deeper
I was meant to love deeper
Deeper, not desperately
I just wanted to be safe and happy
Words jumble up inside
The chaos in my mind is overgrown with weeds
The kind with flowers, thorns, and seeds
The ones that are not so pleasing to see

But they are the medicine I need
Their pricks are honest with me
As I sit in the garden
I breathe deeper
A sigh between cries
A cry between sighs

The growing inside
begins again

Refreshing the seasons
I wanted to be there for the right reasons
The pretty seeds I have watered
drowned
And it put me back
into the ground

Moistening the soil with my tears
Learning once again to crush eggshells
With my hands instead of my feet.

My heart needs time to speak
My mind keeps making me repeat
My tired body doesn't flinch anymore
When my alma tells me that I needed more

More time to grow
More time to heal
More time to speak

Time, trailing off and transcending
I had to remember what love I was tending
No one could tell you how move that energy
What once was a barren ground
Now meant to be
Filled with sprouts of springtime
Scents of pheromones and feminine energy
Laugher escaping like smoke
Light at the end of this moment

I sit in my garden of weeds
Where the birds and bees sing
My alma spoke to me
In the wind and in the breeze
I never paid much attention
To the small moments
Abruptly changing inside of me

But today I listened
As I sit in my garden of weeds
With herbs that heal my needs
As wind howls and I breathe
El viento llevando el humo pesado
de amor que atormenta
sobre mi cabeza
Viento
Dame claridad y certeza
Hablame viento
Leave me with pain I must feel
So I may truly begin to heal
And begin to nurture the love I should feel
Beginning again like seasons do
As I sit in my garden that heals

Para ti,
self love

Quiero dejarte flores en la mesa
Quiero adorar como te ves en el espejo
Quiero recorrer el mundo contigo
Quiero darte todo lo que quieres
Because you are worth every ounce of passion
I have in my veins;
because without your essence,
your kindness- I wouldn't be here,
because of you:
I love,
I live,
    I live for you.
Alegría.

"Píntate un bosque y piérdete"

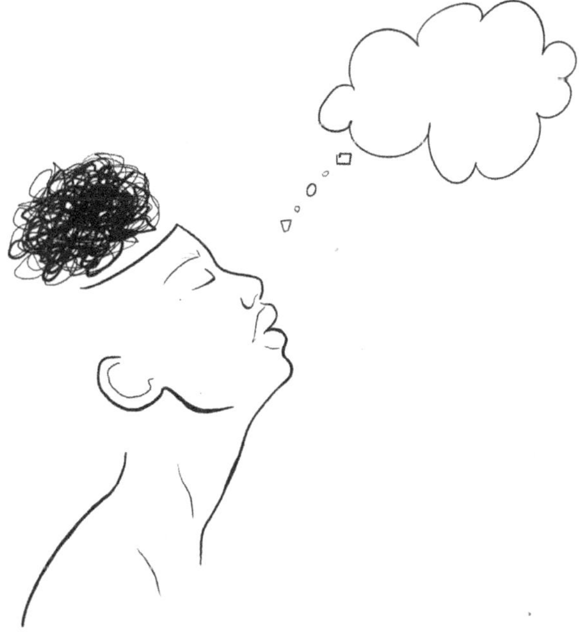

Acknowledgements

For my parents, thank you for nurturing me into the woman I am today.

For my siblings, for always being yourselves and for the love and unbreakable bond we have.

For my friends, who have consistently supported me throughout this journey.

And to my cousin Ana for her Foreword, and my friend Lily whose artwork is showcased throughout the book.

For Davina and Alegría Magazine Familia, thank you for helping me unlock the potential of my inner artist.

To you, Thank you for choosing this book, my first of many.

Cheers to you.

Biography

Alegría, the emotion she was given as a name. Alegría Zuluaga is a proud multi- ethnic woman- orgullosamente (proudly) Colombian, Mexican and Indonesian. She is a hopeless romantic, a gardener, and cultivator of sueños through her writing. A writer and an advocate for education through literature and art.

Alegría is currently a student at California State University of Long Beach working on her Bachelors and double majoring in Comparative World Literature and Linguistics. Her love for language and culture has always been a big motivator for her wandering spirit.

Before she started hopping on planes halfway across the world by herself, her first experiences of travel through space and time were through books. As a child, Alegria had her nose stuck in stories, knitting in grade school, and singing opera. Some say she's an old soul. Her love for literature was nurtured by her father, who never had a TV but an armour full of novels, poetry, and philosophy.

"Every child is an artist. The problem is how to remain an artist once he grows up." *-Picasso*.

In the summer of 2018, she took a volunteer opportunity to teach children in San Miguel Tucuman, Argentina. This is where she quickly learned that creating art serves grounding in the midst of chaos. Art returns one to their inner child, and the innocent hunger to create magic occurs.

In her free time, you can find her dancing in her garden or singing in the kitchen with a wooden spoon as her microphone. She indulges herself in nature and loves getting lost in new places. Alegría is 23 years old and is just getting started on her dreams and hopes you are starting on yours too.